Slovakia in Poems

Edited by Eleni Cay
2021

'SLOVAKIA IN POEMS' © 2021
Edited by Eleni Cay © 2021
Translated by: Professor Marián Andričík and Eleni Cay

Published by Global Slovakia, Bratislava, Slovakia
Co-published with Hybrid Global Publishing,
301 E 57th street, 4th FL, New York, NY 10022 USA
All rights reserved

No part of this book may be reproduced or transmitted in any form or by any means electronic or mechanical, including photocopying, recording or by any information storage and retrieval system, without permission in writing form from the publisher.

Front and back cover design: Ivana Štigová
Photographs: Ivana Štigová

Manufactured in Slovakia for the Slovak market, the United States of America for the US market, or in the United Kingdom when distributed elsewhere.

ISBN: 978-1-7374054-1-2
Library of Congress cataloging-in-publication data available upon request
www.globalslovakia.com

CONTENTS

Foreword - *James Ragan*...1

Košice - *Mark Chamberlain*..7

Košice - *Mark Chamberlain*..8

Ode to Bratislava Rolls - *Robert Peake*..10

Óda na bratislavské rožky - *Robert Peake*...11

Three Blue Mountains - *John Glenday*..13

Tri modré vrchy - *John Glenday*...14

Reading the signs - *Anne-Marie Fyfe*..15

Čítanie znakov - *Anne-Marie Fyfe*..16

After - *Cahal Dallat*..17

Po - *Cahal Dallat*..19

In a Bratislava bar, I am told - *Christina Thatcher*............................22

V bratislavskom bare mi hovoria - *Christina Thatcher*.......................23

Learning to write poetry - *Catherine Davidson*..................................27

Učím sa písať poéziu - *Catherine Davidson*......................................29

I apply for the Slovakian TEFL course - *Miranda Peake*....................31

Uchádzam sa o slovenský kurz vyučovania angličtiny ako cudzieho jazyka - *Miranda Peake*..32

Chlieb s Reďkovkou at Ars Poetica 13..33

Chlieb s reďkovkou na Ars Poetica 13..34

Flow - *Theresa Sowerby*..35

Prúd - *Theresa Sowerby*..37

Sleep-bringer - *Penny Sharman*..39

Uspávač - *Penny Sharman*...41

AKA Silvertown - *Mark Niel*..44

Známa aj ako strieborné mesto - *Mark Niel*.............................47

Živánska - *James Ragan*...49

Živánska - *James Ragan*...51

THE GREAT UNSUNG OF BRATISLAVA - *Matthew Paul*..................53

VEĽKÍ NEOSLAVOVANÍ BRATISLAVČANIA - *Matthew Paul*...............55

Gale over Slovak Paradise - *Elaine Baker*................................57

Víchrica nad Slovenským rajom - *Elaine Baker*........................59

A Letter to the Admiral of the Fleet - *Matt Barnard*...................61

List admirálovi flotily - *Matt Barnard*.......................................63

Absinthe Punch in Bratislava - *Simon Barraclough*.....................65

Absintový punč v Bratislave - *Simon Barraclough*......................67

Below the Tatra Mountains - *Tera Vale Ragan*.........................69

Pod Tatrami - *Tera Vale Ragan*..71

Foreword to the Anthology "Slovakia in Poems"
by James Ragan

In 1969 in Duquesne, Pennsylvania, as a teenager I sat with my family in breathless anticipation in front of a TV screen, as an American rocket lifted from its pad to begin its voyage through space to where two humans would first step onto the surface of the moon. It was a day of celebration as I, myself, prepared that very evening to be the first of my family to make my own maiden flight to visit my parents' villages of Černina and Turcovce near Humenné in Southeastern Slovakia from where they immigrated in 1929 at the peak of a global Depression. And what great news I had to share with my Slovak cousins. Little did I know during my first Živánska on a village hilltop beneath a full moon, that when I pointed into space to exclaim, "Do you believe at this very moment, two American astronauts are walking on the moon!" that my words would be met with derisive laughter. "Dear cousin Jakub" they responded, "the Russians landed a man on the moon years ago."

It was my first personal understanding of the power of propaganda and the cultural mind suppression that would bind fast to an entire generation of my village relatives who had survived the Nazis during the 2nd World War and the Communist coup of 1948, whose dogmatic socialist realism caused a post-war stagnation that would last for generations. It was also the beginning of my many years of dissent in writing poems against the totalitarian rule of the insipidly cruel and despotic Soviet domination of a once proud democratic country.

Speaking Slovak at home until my parents had passed, I had been groomed in the "old country" traditions through its music, art, and literature-- Bednár, Tatarka, Blažková -- and while fellow Slovak, Andy Warhol, was studying art in Pittsburgh, we boasted of his family origins, only 20 miles from my parents' villages, as well as of Ladislav Grossman's "Shop on Main Street," whose images for the Oscar winning film, were based on his hometown of Humenne, only 5 miles away. During my many visits, I dedi-cated myself to a literary life, determined to document the socialist period of Novotny's rule of censorship and imprisonment, through the lens of witnesses who had survived the oppression leading up to the 1968 Soviet invasion of Czechoslovakia, and to the fall of the Berlin Wall in 1989.

For my part, during a Fulbright Professorship in Slovenia, I was invited to give a samizdat candlelight reading in a Bratislava basement on my way to the villages. I was asked by the US Em-bassy to smuggle 10 Newsweek and 10 Time magazines in a "false bottom" suitcase to distribute to the attending poets. I was in awe, as they shoved and pushed to get to the magazines, in ef-fect, "grabbing for truth." That moment predicted the literary challenges awaiting me, as my book, In the Talking Hours, with poems praising Ján Palach and excoriating the presence of Russian tanks in Humenné, was banned, requiring me to sign in at police stations when visiting cities in Czechoslovakia. At a local library, I was called in to witness poems being scissored from my book, which was then re-shelved, wounded, but breathing.

These accounts represent my experience in a Slovakia under communist rule, before political "freedoms" in 1989 inspired once again the exhilaration, through poetry, to "epitomize the open spirit" of Slovakia, echoing Eleni Cay's invitation for readers to experience the country "with all the senses, in an authen-tic personal way." Surely, the artists who survived the pre-1989 period of subjugation cannot escape the lessons of the past as Mark Chamberlain reminds us in his poem, "In Košice," where he translates a stone plaque "in memory of the fighters of fascism / who were hung on this street in January '45." Even one simple image can evoke the nascent Cold War memory of arsenals infil-trating our psyches, as SJ Fowler walks us down the Danube to sit in a Botanical garden, and at a "dinopark" with "animatonic dinosaurs... that could only move one appendage. Must have cost a bomb."

But, truly, this is a book of celebration, reminding us that "with freedom, like dreams, comes responsibility" (sorry to mutate the famous dictum). The international voices in this collection, as beneficiaries of artistic freedom, have welcomed the responsibility to ingest through their eyes, voices, and imaginations, not only the memory of the stunning beauty of the country's mountains, lakes, and villages that they visited or inhabited, but also to reflect on the generous hospitality and warm resilient nature of a vibrant Slovak people.

Whether hooking Christmas carp from Zemplínska Šírava in Christina Thatcher's poem, "In a Bratislava Bar, I am told" or enjoying culinary delights through Robert Peake's tasting of glazed "poppy seed" rolls while revelling that in such "etiquette of pastry... isn't this called love, in any language?" Or the witty surreal ru-minations of Simon Barraclough's "Absinthe Punch in Bratislava," whose kaleidoscopic euphoria immerses us at a market stall in a metaphoric "diorama of Mars" whose "red earth made from red cabbage " is "studded with duck legs." Later, a church levitates and "looks like a decorated sugar cake" moving "like a Roomba / through quiet streets at night."

As one can see, a literary anthology, by its nature, assembles a multitude of visions, that by their passions contemplate the dauntingly profound universality of art in fulfilling its soul's survival in history. Even when traumatized by lost freedoms, Slovakia had never lost its dignity and idealism. Thus, Cahal Dallat explores this in his poem "After," which shapes his view of "intersectionality," as the excitement, experienced in the Esterha-zy Palace of art, depicting Jánošík, the legendary Slovak Robin Hood on horseback, soaring over peasants, "weaving seamlessly through Cubism, socialist realism, folk-art and Byzantine orthodoxy as if they'd been there all along."

Legends abound again as Matthew Paul glorifies "The Great Unsung of Bratislava" winning the 1969 European Soccer Cup, only one year after the Warsaw Pact had invaded the city in 1968. With no absence of irony, the losing team "slides about like newborn deer while the other glides over velvet." Consider also the Bathory Legend of the Queen, who bathed in the blood of virgins to retain her youth, as the focus in Eleni Cay's "Royal Beauty.""There was blood...But no beauty...beauty is not made of blood. It is made of time."

The rebirth of freedom is never more thematically married to the power of words than in the book's panorama of artwork, whose sensory tableaus reveal the Slovak pride in the timeless beauty of nature. These qualities are visually realized in "Below the Tatra Mountains" by Tera Vale Ragan, imagining "the change of hues on the patched earth, a world in its wealth of green" and the "bronzed wheat and sunflowers boughing up their necks to the threshed sky;" or in Miranda Peake's power in dream fulfillment, "In every photograph it was August... mountains with turrets and lakes dropped somehow from above;" and in Penny Sharman's "Sleep-Bringer," "Show me your dance from the fields of wind. Feed me your memory of wild freedom to bloom..."

We are gifted with a range of themes on memory and hope. Catherine Davidson's tribute in "Learning to Write Poetry," reminds her, up late in a bar, to "live poetry"..."a lost sense of something swallowed"...and to follow its traces, "All other faiths deserting, this remaining." Mark Niel in "AKA Silvertown" affirms while searching for a place to propose near Banská Štiavnica, that "the kaleidoscopic palette of the forest / the patchwork quilt of coloured leaves and mountain fresh air /soothed his soul and hinted at hope." Theresa Sowerby's "Flow" creates the memory-play and "inward smile" of an "ageless woman," floating "paper boats," like unfulfilled dreams, and yet who, as a "fair-haired girl-child looks boldly ahead."

Vulnerability as a theme takes several forms, first, in Anne-Marie Fyfe's wry forewarning, "Reading the Signs," signaling language hurdles, on a cross-Slovakia sojourn, for foreigners in an auto with a GB sticker, that inspires a border-crossing bribe with "border boys pointing to American jeans? / giving the universal finger-&-thumb rub that signals / the texture of denim, the promise of US dollars." Matt Barnard's "A Letter to the Admiral of the Fleet" feeds on dispassionate bureaucratic condescension regarding an Admiral's health and his fleet's morale "getting down at heart" over a likely doomed "mission." While Elaine Baker's "Gale over Slovak Paradise" reduces the victim caught in a merciless storm to help-less incredulity, "I sensed it: a rattle in the hearts of the pines...When it left, the forest and I were spent... Out in the open the feathered grasses sagged like women who've lost everything."

In these pages, we celebrate poetry's testament to the beauty and personality of a nation in the purest daily expression of its cultural identity. The poets affirm the legacy of a globalization of the arts, where borders and boundaries can be crossed freely to foster multi-culturalism, the true inspiration at the core of this anthology.

In 1994, I was honored to read for President Václav Havel, during the First International PEN Congress convened in a post-Communist country, a recognition of how far a nation's multi-culturalism and artistic freedom had evolved. After I had addressed the audience in Slovak, Havel confided to me on stage, "don't lose that Zemplinska dialect." Once again, my pride in my Slovak heritage soared. I share that same pride now in the poets, represented here, for lifting up their voices with an eloquence befitting the cultural identity of their respective homelands.

Their poems remind us of a responsibility as artists to strive to achieve, through communication, a moral bond between races and tongues, to see ourselves as global citizens, in the spirit of PEN ideals, with an unwaver-ing vision that poetry, like all the arts, will cross borders and time, inspiring a common share in the moral compass of an enlightened world. To that ideal, the heart sings out to nurture a passion for living, for loving, for learning, and for believing in a future, based on universal truths, to which citizens of all generations might aspire. In his poem, "Three Blue Mountains," John Glenday celebrates his personal found truth, that in scaling the highest peak to the summit, "pick your route well, no one but you can climb it...If the path grows all but impossible, you'll know you're on the right track."

And there's very high optimism in that.

James Ragan

Košice
Mark Chamberlain

Wild poppies push to the sun
through a miasma of building dust,
oil freight arrived from the eastern lowland,
smarting heat, on the banks of the Hornád.

In town on the Hlavná, honey tea,
staff skipping between café tables,
the spires of St Elisabeth's, students, love.
A faded plaque on a yellow wall reads:

*In memory of the fighters of fascism
who were hanged on this street in January '45.*

Behind a sliding screen at the station,
Doxy Roksy, Tipos scratch cards, the Pravda.
On the window of the kozmetika,
a graffiti artist's tag: blue, febrile, brilliant.

Košice
Mark Chamberlain

Cez miazmu stavebného prachu
tlačia sa na slnko divé maky.
Olejná preprava dorazila z východnej nížiny,
skľučujúce teplo na brehoch Hornádu.

Medový čaj v centre na Hlavnej,
zamestnanci pobehujú medzi stolmi v kaviarni,
študenti, láska, veže sv. Alžbety.
Vyblednutá tabuľa na žltej stene nesie nápis:

Na pamiatku bojovníkov fašizmu
obesených na tejto ulici v januári '45.

Za posuvnými dvermi na stanici
Doxy Roksy, stieracie žreby Tiposu, Pravda.
Na okne kozmetiky
značka graffiti umelca: modrá, horúčkovitá, žiarivá.

Ode to Bratislava Rolls (having never tasted one)
Robert Peake

You must send me there at once. Despite
being gluten-free, I am sure my stomach
would make an exception. They are shaped
like a horseshoe, which makes them lucky,
unless you hold them upside down, so luck
drains from their sharpened tips, fickle
luck, to be lost as easily as a poppy seed,
with which our eponymous rolls are filled,
I'm told, so avoid taking a drug test or
watching the Wizard of Oz for at least
thirty minutes after eating one. Did I mention
the glaze? Made from the yolks of decorated
eggs, given an honourable discharge before
whisking, to retain the dignified appearance
of marbled gold. Could you wear them
as a bracelet? I don't know the etiquette
of pastry well enough to tell you. I do
know what it's like to pull apart something
beautiful, and find something else inside.
Isn't this called love, in any language?

Óda na bratislavské rožky (ktoré som ani neochutnal)
Robert Peake

Musíš ma ta ihneď poslať. Hoci
mám bezlepkovú diétu, môj žalúdok by isto
urobil výnimku. Majú tvar
konskej podkovy, čo ich robí šťastnými,
kým ich nedržíš naopak, čím šťastie
kvapká z ich zaostrených koncov, vrtkavé
šťastie, stratí sa ľahko ako mak,
ktorým sú naše rovnomenné rožky plnené,
vravia mi, takže vyhnite sa drogovému testu alebo
nesledujte Čarodejníka z krajiny Oz aspoň
pol hodiny po tom, čo ho zjete. Spomenul som
polevu? Urobenú zo žĺtkov kraslíc,
ktoré pred vyšľahaním úctivo
vypustia zo škrupiny, aby si zachovali dôstojný vzhľad
mramorového zlata. Nosili by ste ich
ako náramok? Neovládam dosť dobre etiketu
pečiva, aby som vám poradil. Ale
viem, aké je to roztrhnúť niečo
krásne a nájsť dnu čosi iné.
Nevolá sa to vo všetkých jazykoch láska?

Three Blue Mountains
John Glenday

Three blue mountains under God, that's all we need.
This one was climbed by the writer and his love,
a dirty, dangerous journey, strewn with rubbish and deceit.
Such bravery. They died up there, of course, but they will
always return. They will never not be heard from again.

This one a young woman scaled for the very first time,
on her own, against all odds. The highest peak,
all the way to the top, it was quite a battle. Some say
four men got there before her, but she was really the first.
Who would have believed such things would happen here?

The third is waiting for you. Pick your route well, no one
but you can climb it. The going is steep and certainly
uncertain, but isn't that always the way of it? If the path grows
all but impossible, you'll know you're on the right track.
Make it to the summit, and you'll get to the bottom of things.

Tri modré vrchy
John Glenday

Tri modré vrchy pod Bohom, viac nám netreba.
Na tento vystúpil spisovateľ so svojou láskou,
nepríjemná, nebezpečná cesta, plná odpadkov a ľsti.
Taká statočnosť. Pravdaže, zomreli tam, ale vždy
sa vrátia. Už nebude, že sa viac neozvú.

Tento po prvý raz zliezla mladá žena,
sama, napriek všetkému. Najvyšší štít,
celý výstup až na vrchol bol silný boj. Vraj
sa ta pred ňou dostali štyria muži, ale ona bola ozaj prvá.
Kto by bol veril, že sa tu také čosi prihodí?

Tretí čaká na teba. Dobre si vyber, kadiaľ pôjdeš, nik
naň nemôže vyliezť, iba ty. Výstup je strmý a zaiste
neistý, ale nebýva to tak vždy? Ak sa už ďalej
takmer nebude dať ísť, vieš, že si na správnej ceste.
Vylez až na vrchol, a dostaneš sa na koreň vecí.

Reading the signs
Anne-Marie Fyfe

Josef exploring Volkswagen underside in *Hotel Parking*,
thumbs up messaging through glass, *no devices* — *pirohy*
and *sheep-cheese* (in English) pennants on *Grand Salon*
breakfast buffet — Josef dusting the rear-window GB sticker
— last night's windscreen *vignette* (40 *koruny* at 2am) — frontier
kiosk-blind shoots up, *no smoking no guns* icons, then
cambio closed — today, cue black & white credits flickering
across final fogbound castle scenario into cinema dark
— only sign's a green man sprinting on stairs and — I guess —
Slovak word for *exit* — then paying an old man in a red coat
for postcards near the cathedral — months on, levelling
some wheat-field sunset with a rattling crossroads bicycle
I'm indicating road-map placenames by a river:
the overalled mechanic? farmhand? (I'm reading signs here?)
glances back at silent red-tiled barns, outbuildings,
stone-spire church, sure that he's unobserved talking
at the GB sticker, nods *straight ahead* to a distant neon
gas-station where the clerk is gesturing *fork right* volubly
at the *semaphory* (I translate his traffic-light gesticulation)
towards the military bridge, its low sunbeam flicker,
the *last car wash before border* boys dismissing *koruny*
with a cool shrug, pointing to *American jeans?*,
giving the universal finger-&-thumb rub that signals
the texture of denim, the promise of US dollars.

Čítanie znakov
Anne-Marie Fyfe

Josef skúma podvozok volkswagena na parkovisku hotela,
cez sklo posiela správu palec hore, nič tam nie je — pirohy
a ovčí syr (v angličtine) klubové vlajočky vo Veľkom salóne
bufetové raňajky — Josef čistí prach z nálepky GB na zadnom okne
— diaľničná nálepka zo včera na prednom skle (40 korún o druhej v noci)
— roleta na hraničnom stánku vystrelí nahor - piktogramy zákaz fajčiť,
zákaz zbraní, potom cambio zavreté — dnes sa
čiernobiele záverečné titulky mihajú cez poslednú scénu hradu v hmle
do tmy kina — jediným znakom je zelený muž šprintujúci po schodoch a
— tipujem — slovenský výraz pre exit — potom platíme starcovi v
červenom kabáte pri katedrále za pohľadnice — o niekoľko mesiacov
neskôr dobieham akýsi pšeničný západ slnka na
hrkotajúcom dedinskom bicykli, na automape ukazujem miestne názvy
pri rieke:
mechanik v montérkach? robotník na farme? (čítam tu znaky?)
opätuje letmý pohľad pri tichých stodolách s červenými strechami,
hospodárske budovy, kostol s kamennou vežičkou, je si istý, že ho nik
nepozoruje, keď rozpráva pri nálepke GB, kývne priamo pred seba na
vzdialený neón benzínovej pumpy, kde predavač výrečne gestikuluje na
semaforoch doprava (prekladám jeho semaforovú gestikuláciu)
k vojenskému mostu, na ňom blikot nízkeho slnečného lúča, posledná
autoumyváreň pred hranicou chlapci s chladným pokrčením pliec
odmietajú koruny, ukazujú na americké džínsy?,
šúchajú si ukazovák o palec, čo všade značí rifľovinu, prísľub
amerických dolárov.

After
Cahal Dallat

Ľudovít Fulla,
Slovak National Gallery, Bratislava

Noon, a dry-tongued heat,
after the obligatory castle morning,

a torn-out travel-writer's grudging
account – rough folded in our guide –
finds fault with, he complains,
too-Eastern-bloc housing blocks,
over der schönen blauen Danube,
too numerous post-Communist
ticket-stub-tearers; too-religious
Christs on varnished street-corner
oak crosses; even too-Western
pizzerias, a busker playing
I Just Called...
      All that
intersectionality, that excitement
being exactly what we've come
to find in a visited-for-the-first-time
European capital city.

But all that's as nothing to three
enchanted things in a dim
afternoon Esterházy Palace:

Janosik, the local, the true,
Robin Hood on horseback; a vivid
trumpeter soaring over ploughmen,

*reapers, farm carts; a small red
mother and child*
      weaving seamlessly
through Cubism, socialist realism,
folk-art and Byzantine orthodoxy,
as if they'd been there all along.

Po
Cahal Dallat

Ľudovít Fulla
Slovenská národná galéria Bratislava

Poludnie, z horúčavy peklo v ústach,
po povinnom dopoludní na hrade

vytrhnutá skúpa správa
spisovateľa na cestách – len tak zložená v našom bedekri –
kritizuje, ponosuje sa,
priveľmi východné bloky
nad krásnym modrým Dunajom,
priveľa postkomunistických
trhačov lístkov; priveľmi zbožní
Kristovia na lakovaných dubových krížoch
na rohu ulice; dokonca priveľmi západné
pizzerie, pouličný muzikant, čo hrá
I Just Called...
 Všetka tá
pretínavosť, vzrušenie
je presne tým, čo sme prišli
hľadať v prvý raz navštívenom
európskom hlavnom meste.

Ale toto všetko je nič oproti trom
čarovným veciam v popoludňajšom
šere Esterházyho paláca:

Jánošík, ten miestny skutočný
Robin Hood na koni; živý
hlásateľ vznášajúci sa nad oráčmi,

žnecmi, poľnými kárami; malá červená
matka s dieťaťom,
      čo sa hladko preplietajú
kubizmom, socialistickým realizmom,
ľudovým umením a byzantským pravoslávím,
akoby tam boli od počiatku.

In a Bratislava bar, I am told
Christina Thatcher

common carp are bottom feeders:
they stuff their bellies with gravel,
zooplankton, molluscs. Gorged
on half-dead tiny wrigglers
they swim the Zemplinska Sirava
until restless hooks *hook*
and one is hauled up, slipped
into a plastic bag the size
of a human torso, driven
miles home then set free
in a bathtub of fresh water.
The carp lives there for days
before the Christmas kill.
People stop bathing. Kids pick
names: Matej, Bonifác, Samuel.
Parents compare sizes, teenagers say
they hate the taste of mud. Protestors
stand freezing at fish markets,
shout: Don't play the executioner!
The clock ticks, the carp swims.
The whole family waits
for good luck.

V bratislavskom bare mi hovoria
Christina Thatcher

kapor obyčajný je dnová ryba:
napcháva si brucho štrkom,
zooplanktónom, mäkkýšmi. Požiera
polomŕtve larvičky komárov,
keď pláva v Zemplínskej Šírave,
až sa chytí na nepokojný háčik
a vytiahnu ho hore, šupnú
do plastového vreca veľkosti
ľudského trupu, odvezú kilometre
domov a potom pustia na slobodu
vo vani s čerstvou vodou.
Kapor tam žije celé dni
až do vianočného zabitia.
Ľudia sa prestanú kúpať. Deti vyberajú
mená: Matej, Bonifác, Samuel.
Rodičia porovnávajú veľkosti, tínedžeri vravia,
že neznášajú chuť blata. Protestujúci
postojačky mrznú na rybích trhoch
a vykrikujú: Nehrajte sa na katov!
Hodiny tikajú, kapor pláva.
Celá rodina čaká
na šťastie.

Royal beauty
(written in response to the Bathory Legend at the Cachtice Castle[1], Slovakia)
Eleni Cay

There was blood. A lot of blood.
But no beauty.
Because beauty is not made of blood,
It is made of time,
it can't be hustled from its bearers,
it behaves like love.

The Cachtice ruins sink into the soil,
autumn leaves enclose the relic in a golden frame.
Ginger-crimson glitters abandon the leaves,
infuse their aches into butterfly wings,
then powder themselves into sunsets.

---

[1] The legend goes that Bathory had vampire-like tendencies and bathed in the blood of virgins to retain her youth and beauty.

Kráľovská krása
(napísané v reakcii na legendu o Báthoryčke[2] na Čachtickom zámku)
Eleni Cay

Tiekla krv. Veľa krvi.
No krásy nikde.
Lebo krása nevzniká z krvi,
vzniká z času,
nemožno ju vynútiť od jej nositeľov,
správa sa ako láska.

Zrúcaniny Čachtického hradu sa vnárajú do zeme,
jesenné lístie rúbi relikviu v zlatom ráme.
Hrdzavo-karmínové ozdoby sa vzdávajú lístia,
vlievajú svoje túžby do motýlích krídel
a potom sa rozprášia do západov slnka.

---

[2] Podľa legendy mala Báthoryčka upírske sklony a kúpavala sa v krvi panien, aby si udržala mladosť a krásu.

Learning to write poetry
Catherine Davidson

I was ten the first time, handed a pen, paper
dawn in the Mojave walking in silence.
The monks led us in a file to an oasis.
A rattlesnake lettered itself over the sand.
Given permission, the world cracked open,
pink sky singing, an egg-shaped bell broken.

At twelve, my grandfather of commerce
unschooled reader, book lover, strike breaker,
soft-spoken tamer of women, cars and horses
offered me gifted Walt Whitman, shirt parted,
eyes like a token, his bridge over the cosmos,
as inviting and simple as a girl's first passion.

At fifteen, I entered into the life of the body:
lines under fingernails, muddy and stinking,
men a foreign tongue I longed to master, scent
leading me into the underworld, undrowned.
I fell for a dead Greek among other seducers.
Each time a word pierced me I was done over.

A decade on, together in a room for hours,
the brilliant teacher and his acolytes, up late
in the bar, a Slovak who shouldered worlds,
said we should live poetry but what did I know?
Poems walked through me and out the door
on their way to other cities, other chances.

Nights during the years of children, I woke,
stood at the landing looking at the moon,
or in the car watched a plane split the sky.
Poetry a lost sense of something swallowed.
Pebbles thrown into water, I followed traces.
All other faiths deserting me, this remaining:

a cedar only I can see, evergreen, verdant
breaking the bare ground of my disunions.

Učím sa písať poéziu
Catherine Davidson

Mala som prvý raz desať, dali mi pero, papier,
na úsvite kráčala ticho Mohavskou púšťou.
Mnísi nás viedli v zástupe do oázy.
Štrkáč sa v piesku zvinul do písmena.
Keď svet dostal povolenie, s praskotom sa otvoril,
ružová obloha zaspievala nad rozbitým vajcovitým zvonom.

Keď som mala dvanásť, môj starý otec obchodník,
neškolený čitateľ, milovník kníh, štrajkokaz,
zmierlivý krotiteľ žien, áut a koní,
mi ponúkol nadaného Walta Whitmana s rozhrnutou košeľou,
očami ako mince, mostom nad vesmírom,
lákavého a prostého ako prvá vášeň dievčaťa.

V pätnástich som vstúpila do života tela:
čiary pod nechtami, hnedasté a páchnuce,
muži, cudzí jazyk, ktorý som túžila zvládnuť, zápach,
ktorý ma viedol so podsvetia, neutopenú.
Spomedzi ostatných zvodcov som sa zaľúbila do mŕtveho Gréka.
Zakaždým, keď ma prebodlo slovo, som bola hotová.

O desaťročie neskôr, celé hodiny spolu v izbe,
skvelý učiteľ a jeho nasledovníci, do noci
v bare, Slovák, čo niesol na pleciach svety,
povedal, mali by sme žiť poéziu, ale čo som vedela?
Básne prešli cezo mňa a von z dverí
na ceste k iným mestám, iným príležitostiam.

Počas rokov, keď som už mala deti, som sa v noci zobúdzala,
stála na podeste a hľadela na mesiac

alebo v aute sledovala, ako lietadlo delí oblohu.
Poézia, stratený zmysel čohosi potlačeného.
Okruhliaky hodené do vody, šla som po stopách.
Všetky ostatné viery ma zradili, táto zostáva:

céder, ktorý vidím len ja, vždy zelený, svieži,
rozrýva holú zem mojich rozkolov.

I apply for the Slovakian TEFL course
Miranda Peake

I had thought I could do it, move my life to the heat
of the landlocked sun. In every photograph it was August and
that was part of it, but not the whole.
There were the mountains with turrets and lakes dropped somehow
from above. When I dreamt it from my desk I was
up early most days books in a bag, people
to teach, although of course I am an introvert and teaching
would've been impossible or agony, but these
were dreams.

Uchádzam sa o slovenský kurz vyučovania angličtiny ako cudzieho jazyka
Miranda Peake

Myslela som, že to zvládnem, premiestniť svoj život do horúčavy
vnútrozemského slnka. Na každej fotografii bol august a
to bola len časť, no nie všetko.

Boli tam aj hory s vežičkami a jazierkami akosi zhodenými
zhora. Keď som o tom snívala od stola, väčšinu
dní som vstávala zavčasu, knihy v taške, ľudia,
ktorých mám učiť, hoci som, samozrejme, introvert a učiť
by som nemohla alebo by som prežívala muky, ale to
boli sny.

Chlieb s Reďkovkou at Ars Poetica 13

You have to admit, says the man as he bikes away
we're not a cultured nation. So we named it, and now what?
       Zuzana Husarova

SJ Fowler

I was re-upped early again
and walked an hour or two to down the Danube
before cutting in to the outskirts to visit.
I sit down and there's children there. It's that easy. I'm relatively
fertile.

The Botanical gardens, and then one of the best zoos I ever
visited.
I got quite emotional meeting the bear.
I had to touch a baby meerkat.
There was a white tiger and a red panda.
The whole thing was mental.

What overheard conversation is a visitor
to a small place from a water weighted burying action?
I like folk music but cannot follow electronic performance.
How can I judge? I am from a whack of land.

And they had a dinopark, it was animatronic dinosaurs
that could only move one appendage.
Must have cost a bomb.
So weird it was one of the happiest mornings I can remember,
pumped on coffee, watching babies be emergent, music in,
animals right in my fat.

Chlieb s reďkovkou na Ars Poetica 13

Musíš uznať, vraví muž, keď odchádza na bicykli, že nie sme kultúrny národ, tak sme to pomenovali, a čo teraz?
Zuzana Husárová

SJ Fowler

Dal som sa ráno znova dokopy
a zo dve hodiny som kráčal popri Dunaji,
potom som zaskočil na predmestie na návštevu.
Sadám si a sú tam deti. Je to také ľahké. Som relatívne plodný.

Botanická záhrada a jedna z najlepších ZOO, akú som kedy navštívil.
Celkom ma dojalo stretnutie s medveďom.
Musel som sa dotknúť malej surikáty.
Bol tam biely tiger a panda červená.
Celé to bolo bláznivé.

Aký rozhovor môže náhodne započuť návštevník
malého mesta z kraja, ktorý pochováva váha vody?
Mám rád ľudovú hudbu, ale nemôžem počúvať elektronické verzie. Ako to viem posúdiť? Som z veľkej krajiny.

A mali aj dinopark, boli tam animatronické dinosaury,
ktoré mohli pohybovať len jednou časťou.
Muselo to stáť majland.
Bolo to také zvláštne, jedno z najšťastnejších dopoludní, aké pamätám,
naliaty kávou som sledoval, ako sa liahnu mláďatá, s hudbou,
zvieratá rovno pred mojou tučnou tvárou.

Flow
Theresa Sowerby

Klimt fabric woodland forms a shower curtain
behind her bath with its floating paper boats.
This is where our story starts.

But look again. There are people in the boats – couples,
someone waving, one lone figure shadow-black.
You're getting the picture.

Look again. Is she playing? She holds a boat in her right hand.
Her left touches a reed. But why is her hair blue, bound
and such a weight?

Look how big she is. No child. An ageless woman, loaded
with thought in a shallow river, anchored by gravity,
longing to be swept away.

*

Later she dreams her hair a yellow cocoon. She is pregnant
with paper boats, carries their sailors within her. Two shadows now,
one dangling its legs, one trailing a hand in the water.

Turtle-like limbs propel her past fishes and fronds of weed.
An inward smile relaxes her face. Guiding the fleet, a fair-haired
girl-child looks boldly ahead.

Later she dreams her hair a yellow cocoon. She is pregnant
with paper boats, carries their sailors within her. Two shadows now,
one dangling its legs, one trailing a hand in the water.

Turtle-like limbs propel her past fishes and fronds of weed.

An inward smile relaxes her face. Guiding the fleet, a fair-haired girl-child looks boldly ahead.

Prúd
Theresa Sowerby

Látka s Klimtovým lesom tvorí sprchový záves
za jej vaňou s plávajúcimi papierovými loďkami.
Tu sa začína náš príbeh.

Prizrite sa však lepšie. V loďkách sú ľudia – páry,
ktosi máva, akási osamotená matnočierna postava.
Už začínate chápať.

Pozrite sa ešte raz. Nehrá sa azda? V pravej ruke drží loďku.
Ľavou sa dotýka tŕstia. Ale prečo má vlasy modré, zviazané
a také ťažké?

Pozri, aká je veľká. Už nie je dieťa. Večne mladá žena, plná
myšlienok v plytkej rieke, s kotvou príťažlivosti,
s túžbou byť uchvátená.

*

Neskôr sníva, vlasy žltý zámotok. Korytnačie
ruky a nohy plávajú medzi rybami a vejármi buriny.
Je tehotná papierovými loďkami,

nesie v sebe ich námorníkov. Dva tiene, jeden pohojdáva
nohami, druhý ťahá ruku vo vode. Plavovlasé dievčatko
na čele flotily sa smelo díva vpred.

Neskôr sníva, vlasy žltý zámotok. Je tehotná
papierovými loďkami, nesie v sebe ich námorníkov. Dva tiene,
jeden pohojdáva nohami, druhý ťahá ruku vo vode.

Korytnačie ruky ju ženú popri rybách a vejároch buriny.
Vnútorný úsmev jej uvoľňuje tvár. flotily.
Plavovlasé dievčatko na čele
flotily sa smelo díva vpred.

Sleep-bringer [1]
Penny Sharman

I found you
in the Botanical garden
far from
your native landscapes,
white petticoats,
paper petals,
tall and strong,
purple centre
of mountain ranges.

I heard your
giant rattle heads,
song of tiny white seeds,
hill lover, peace flower,
shade of pure white.
I tasted you
on the crust,
sweet nutty oil.

I think
you're safe.
I'll pretend
you're not addictive.
Moon potion,
bedtime chutney
send me
dreams from
Hekate Goddess
of flower law.
I bow down.

Bring me
my dreamtime
from your white skirts
and lavender stories.
Show me
your dance
from the fields of wind.

Feed me
your memory
of wild,
freedom to bloom,
give me
your blessed drug
of small seeds.

[1] Elka Crone Poppy
Papaver Somniferum

Uspávač [2]
Penny Sharman

Našla som ťa
v botanickej záhrade,
ďaleko od
tvojho rodného kraja,
biele sukničky,
papierové lupienky,
vysoké a silné,
purpurový stred
horských hrebeňov.

Počula som tvoje
obrovské hrkálky,
pieseň bielych semienok,
mierový kvietok či milovník úbočí,
odtieň čistej bieloby.
Ochutnala som ťa
na kôrke,
sladký orechový olej.

Myslím,
že si bezpečný.
Budem predstierať,
že nie si návykový.
Mesačný elixír,
čatní na dobrú noc,
pošli mi
sny od
Hekaty bohyne
zákona kvetín.

Skláňam sa.
Prines mi
môj čas stvorenia
zo svojich bielych sukní
a levanduľových príbehov.
Ukáž mi
svoj tanec
z veterných polí.

Nakŕm ma
svojou divou
pamäťou,
slobodou kvitnúť,
daj mi
svoj požehnaný liek
z malých semienok.

[2] Mak siaty
Papaver Somniferum

AKA Silvertown
Mark Niel

Something strange and wonderful:
the kaleidoscopic palette of the forest,
the patchwork quilt of coloured leaves and mountain fresh air
soothed his soul and hinted at hope,
after this longest and hardest of summers.

Two buses and six hours from Vienna,
he was welded to his seat.
He prised himself up and out,
stood and stretched, like a mainspring
unwinding the kinks travel had bequeathed him.

This was Banská Štiavnica (he pronounced it Banská Something),
in spite of repeated attempts by Slovaks
to educate his lazy Anglo-Saxon ears.
It didn't worry him, for music was his Lingua Franca.
He headed for the Visitor Centre, bearing his burning questions.

Which cafes sell the best coffee and might buy his act?
He'd play for tips, a meal and a sofa for sleep.
He'd bluff the love songs, singing heavy-hearted since
she'd left him in Budapest, weary of his drifter ways
unaware he was searching for the perfect place to propose.

His dwindling stash of cash was the last from the pawned ring.
So now he needs to sing, to unburden, unload,
let strangers feel the danger of this unanchored boat,
hands, guitar and lips in synchrony emote,
desperate to keep his sinking soul afloat.

Yet, there is still magic made in this town.
His keening songs hit true and hit home
with one whose heartache matched his own.
One year later, in wedding suit and gown
Each declared in each other, their fortune found, in Silvertown.

Známa aj ako strieborné mesto
Mark Niel

Čosi zvláštne a nádherné:
kaleidoskopická paleta lesa,
zošívaná deka z farebných listov a čerstvý horský vzduch
uľavili jeho duši a dali štipku nádeje
po tomto najdlhšom a najťažšom z liet.

Dva autobusy a šesť hodín z Viedne
bol privarený k sedadlu.
Ťahal sa hore, do strán,
vstával, preťahoval sa ako hlavná pružina
a rozmotával slučky, čo mu zanechalo cestovanie.

Toto bola Banská Štiavnica (vyslovil to Banská Čosi),
napriek opakovanému úsiliu Slovákov
vyškoliť jeho lenivé anglosaské uši.
Netrápilo ho to, lebo jeho lingua franca bola hudba.
Namieril si to do informačného strediska so svojimi súrnymi
otázkami.

Kde majú najlepšiu kávu a kde by mohli kúpiť jeho predstavenie?
Hrá za prepitné, jedlo a nocľah.
Predstiera ľúbostné piesne, spieva ich skľúčený, odkedy
ho v Budapešti nechala, unavená z jeho tuláckych ciest,
nevediac, že hľadá najlepšie miesto na žiadosť o ruku.

Jeho scvrkávajúce sa zásoby hotovosti boli posledné
zo založeného prsteňa.
A tak teraz musí spievať, sňať bremeno, vyliať si srdce,
nech cudzinci pocítia nebezpečenstvo tohto neukotveného člna,
ruky, gitara a pery sa naraz citmi plnia
v zúfalej túžbe, nech mu klesajúcu dušu nepotopí vlna.

A predsa sa v tomto meste tvoria zázraky.
Jeho clivé piesne našli cieľ a zasiahli
niekoho, kto nemal o nič menej trápení.
O rok nato, vo svadobnom zladení
dali si sľub tam, v striebornom meste svojej šťasteny.

Živánska
James Ragan

*...the meal the Slovak folk hero Janosik
ate in the forest while on the run.*

After the doors were shut and the windows sealed
to let the ember's soft foot lie, my father
slapped the crystal clear of wine, and rising
tall as Janosik, full of heart, whispered down,

"Grass is burning. Stags are in the wood."

And out into the green night and salt arbors
of the brook we followed the king of bandits
upslope through the branched spires and thickets
into the forest where only mold and roses thorned.

Under a moon as low as a mushroom scone,
we soured coals in sprigs and ginger grass,
and hidden as with any fear the mind deceives to rob,
the sparks saw into the burning earth

what flint of fire could set the night to gasp.
A crackling sound began to grow into the roaring
hooves of deer and longer still to racing herds
as bacon fat dripped longingly into laps of bread,

and onions skewered and spat above the fire spears.
In my father's fist the long wind reed became a switch
that like the last finger on a hand hooked
potatoes by the eye. Wine took the aching down
into the throat and further in, the heart of something

shook that only nature recognized as sound.
The grass had burned to snapping darkness and to the last sobbing tongue, my father pointed down,

"The stags are gone. Boars have killed their young."

And no one moved. The king of bandits sheathed
his spearhead into ground. None had known
that hidden behind the wet rock of the August clearing
a boar, alone and sorry for its breed, had moaned and wept.

Živánska
James Ragan

... jedlo, ktoré v lese na úteku jedol
slovenský ľudový hrdina Jánošík...

Keď boli dvere pozatvárané a okná utesnené,
aby jemný popol z uhlíkov dotlel, otec
potľapkal po krištáľovočistom víne, vzpriamil sa,
vysoký ako Jánošík, plný nadšenia, a zašepkal:

„Tráva horí. Jelene sú v lese."

A von do zelenej noci a k stromom
pri potoku sme šli za kráľom zbojníkov
hore brehom pomedzi rozvetvené kmene a húštie
do lesa, kde pichala len pôda a ruže.

Pod mesiacom nízko ako klobúčik huby
ochladzovali sme uhlíky vetvičkami a zázvorovou trávou
a iskry, skryté ako v strachu, ktorý myseľ ulúpi klamom,
skúmali v rozpálenej zemi,

aký pazúrik by mohol z noci vykresať ston.
Praskavý zvuk začalo pohlcovať dunenie
kopýt lesnej zveri a ešte dlhšie uháňajúcich čried,
keď do náručia chleba túžobne odkvapkával tuk zo slaniny

a cibuľa napichnutá na ražni prskala nad ohňom.
V otcovej ruke sa dlhá trstina zmenila na prút,
čo ako posledný prst na ruke vytiahol
zemiaky za klíček. Víno vzalo bolesť

do hrdla a odtiaľ ďalej, stred čohosi
sa zatriasol tak, že len príroda to rozpoznala ako zvuk.
Tráva zhorela do praskajúcej tmy a posledného
vzlykajúceho jazyka, otec ukázal dole:

„Jelene sú preč. Diviaky im skántrili mladé."

A nik sa ani nepohol. Kráľ zbojníkov vybral kopiju
a zapichol ju do zeme. Nik nevedel,
že za mokrou skalou na augustovej čistinke skrytý
diviak, sám a v smútku nad svojím druhom stoná a plače.

THE GREAT UNSUNG OF BRATISLAVA
Matthew Paul

European Cup Winners' Cup Final, 1969:
FC Barcelona 2, Slovan Bratislava 3

The scoreline barely tells the story. Straight from kick-off,
Barça—world-famous Barça—see their game-plan erased:
they're outrun, outmanoeuvred, outplayed & demoralised
by Slovan's Total Football avant la lettre: one outfit slides

about like newborn deer while the other glides over velvet.
Just two minutes in, a nutmeg, dummy & run at the petrified
defenders yield Cvetler a goal of utter magnificence. A soft
equaliser is merely tiresome. Hrivnák replies unstoppably:

a high-speed one-two, fortunate deflection & reflex finish.
You make your own luck, coach Vičan maintains afterwards.
Soon Slovan cream a third: Čapkovič surges from the left,
unfurls a dreamy right-foot instep curler beyond the keeper.

Second half, Barça narrow the deficit, direct from a corner.
Forty minutes to go, but the outcome is seldom imperilled.
Slovan caress the ball as if Vičan would wield a cattle-prod
were they to lose it. Truly, they ought to score six or seven.

So ends Europe's first East–versus–West final, in sensibly
neutral Basel. Two pitch-invaders' banner reads, Welcome
& win! Euphoria brings other Bratislava fans onto the turf,
chairing on their shoulders the captain, Alexander Horváth:

arms akimbo & bare-chested like his teammates, imperious
at the centre of chaos. The moment comes: he leads a count

up to three & roars; lifts the cup & glugs some fizz from it,
with the square-jawed insouciance of a film star admiring
in a barber's mirror the sharpest haircut he will ever have.

VEĽKÍ NEOSLAVOVANÍ BRATISLAVČANIA
Matthew Paul

Európsky Pohár víťazov pohárov 1969:
FC Barcelona – Slovan Bratislava 2:3

Výsledok veľmi nezodpovedá priebehu. Hneď po výkope
Barca – svetoznáma Barca – vidí, ako sa rúca jej herný plán:
predbehne, prevýši, zatieni a demoralizuje ich totálny futbal Slovana,
keď sa tomu tak ešte nehovorilo: jeden tím sa šmýka ako novonarodená

srna, kým druhý sa kĺže po zamate. Už po dvoch minútach jasličky,
predstieraná prihrávka a beh pri ústupe vydesených obrancov, Cvetler,
gól, absolútna nádhera. Ľahký vyrovnávajúci je čistá nuda. Hrivnák ne-
zastaviteľne odpovedá:

rýchlovka na 1:2, šťastný teč a reflexívne zakončenie.
Každý si je strojcom svojho šťastia, tvrdí vzápätí tréner Vičan.
Čoskoro Slovan pridáva tretí: Čapkovič sa nahrnie zľava,
priehlavkom pravačky naservíruje nádhernú krútenú za brankára.

Druhý polčas, Barca znižuje náskok priamo z rohu.
Štyridsať minút do konca, ale výsledok je zriedka ohrozený.
Slovan sa mazná s loptou, akoby mal Vičan v ruke bodec na kravy,
ak by to mali prehrať. Fakt, mohli dať šesť či sedem.

Tak sa končí prvé európske finále Východ – Západ v rozumne
neutrálnom Bruseli. Na ihrisko vtrháva dvojica s transparentom Vitajte
a víťazte! Ďalší bratislavskí fanúšikovia sa v eufórii valia na trávnik a na
pleciach nesú kapitána Alexandra Horvátha:

s rukami vbok a s odhalenou hruďou ako jeho spoluhráči, veliteľsky
uprostred chaosu. Prichádza tá chvíľa: napočíta
do troch a vykríkne, dvihne pohár a glgne si z neho šampusu

s energickou nonšalantnosťou filmovej hviezdy kochajúcej sa
u holiča v zrkadle tomu najštýlovejšiemu účesu, aký kedy bude mať.

Gale over Slovak Paradise
Elaine Baker

They taught us in school:
hurricanes don't wrap themselves in seas
and go quietly; they change colour, mutate.
Being landlocked doesn't make us safe.

Playing in the woods, I sensed it:
a rattle in the hearts of the pines,
shudder in the roots.
These trees can't shield us from everything.

The woodcutter warned
RUN. But I was already lost
in branches and needles and earth.
The heavy hand of the wind came, a deep shout,
the longest breath. I thought it would never give out.
On the plain, the grasses and bellflowers were crushed flat.
The forest thrashed,
bruised lilies cried out. The gale tore at the ravine's throat;
waterfalls split. I was pinned to a trunk,
long hair crashing, black as the waves from the hurricane's birthplace.

When it left,
the forest and I were spent and gashed, limbs disjointed.
Out in the open, the feathered grasses sagged
like women who've lost everything,

their white seeds stripped off,
caught in the fur on a wolf's back,
carried to pitch wet caves, deep in silence and salt.

Víchrica nad Slovenským rajom
Elaine Baker

V škole nás učili:
hurikány sa neschovávajú v moriach
a prichádzajú ticho; menia farbu, mutujú.
To, že sme vo vnútrozemí, neznamená bezpečie.

Pri hre v horách som to pocítila:
hrmot v srdciach borovíc,
chvenie v koreňoch.
Tieto stromy nás neochránia pred všetkým.

Drevorubač nás varoval:
UTEKAJTE. No ja som už bola stratená
v konároch, ihličí a hline.
Prišla ťažká ruka vetra, hlboký výkrik,

ten najdlhší nádych. Myslela som, že nikdy neochabne.
Tráva a zvončeky na pláni boli zrovnané so zemou. Les rozdrvený,
dotlčené ľalie kričali. Víchrica sa zahryzla do hrdla rokliny;
vodopád sa rozpolil. Bola som pripichnutá ku kmeňu stromu,
okolo mňa plieskali dlhé vlasy, čierne ako vlny z rodiska hurikánu.

Keď ustala,
i les, i ja sme boli vyčerpaní, údy vykĺbené.
Na čistine ochabnuté chocholaté trávy
ako ženy, ktoré prišli o všetko,

ich biele semená vyzlečené,
zachytené v srsti na chrbte vlka,
nesené do tmavých vlhkých jaskýň,
hlboko do ticha a soli.

A Letter to the Admiral of the Fleet
Matt Barnard

Dear Admiral, your country, as always,
sends its best wishes and thanks you
for your brave and unflinching service.
The sons and daughters of our great state
forever have a place in the people's heart,
and we look forward to the day of your return.

The Ministry of Defence received the returned
life jackets and your note; your advice is always
welcomed and invariably taken to heart
by the Minister and his advisors, though your
tone does not always befit an officer of the state.
The procurement department has served

notice, and we hope the replacements serve
the fleet better. They should arrive by return
of post. We are concerned about the reported state
of your other equipment and note that in all ways
we are ready to support our personnel and you
in your endeavours, which are close to our hearts.

We hope the fleet is not getting down at heart.
We appreciate the conditions in which you all serve
and anticipate a transformation shortly. And you,
dear Admiral, how do you fair? I must return
to the subject, though it seems we are always
straying into this delicate area, but the state

of your health is in this case a matter of state
importance. I refer not only to the physical heart;

the morale of the rank and file will always
reflect that of its commander, which serves
as a reminder to the Ministry in turn
that it is duty of the Minister to provide you

with the vision and leadership that you
deserve. As such, the enclosed leaflets state
in clear terms your mission, and when you return
victorious you will know in your heart
that you have rendered this nation a great service
which will be remembered forever and always.

Be assured, Admiral, we are always thinking of you,
we recognise your service and your value to our state;
your heart will be full when eventually you return.

Yours etc.

List admirálovi flotily
Matt Barnard

Milý pán admirál, krajina vám
ako vždy posiela srdečný pozdrav a ďakuje vám
za statočnú a neochvejnú službu.
Synovia a dcéry tohto veľkého štátu
budú mať navždy miesto v srdciach ľudu
a tešíme sa na deň vášho návratu.

Ministerstvo obrany dostalo vrátené
záchranné vesty a váš list; minister a jeho
poradcovia vaše odporúčanie vítajú
a natrvalo si berú k srdcu, hoci jeho
tón je nie vždy primeraný pozícii štátneho úradníka.
Sekcia zásobovania dala

avízo a dúfame, že vymenené kusy poslúžia
flotile lepšie. Mali by prísť
obratom. Znepokojuje nás hlásený stav
vášho ďalšieho výstroja a sme pripravení
všemožne podporovať vás a vašu posádku
vo vašich počinoch, takých blízkych našim srdciam.

Dúfame, že flotila neklesá na duchu.
Vážime si, za akých podmienok všetci slúžite,
a čoskoro očakávame zmenu. A vy,
milý admirál, ako sa máte? Musím sa vrátiť
k meritu veci, hoci sa zdá, že stále
zabŕdame do tej chúlostivej záležitosti, ale váš

zdravotný stav je v tomto prípade záležitosťou celoštátneho
významu. Nemám na mysli len fyzické zdravie;

morálka mužstva bude vždy
odrážať morálku ich veliteľa, čo
ministerstvu na druhej strane pripomína,
že je povinnosťou ministra vám poskytnúť

víziu a vedenie, aké si
zaslúžite. Priložené brožúrky ako také jasne
stanovujú vaše úlohy, a keď sa víťazne
vrátite, budete v duši cítiť,
že ste tejto krajine preukázali veľkú službu,
ktorú si budeme na veky vekov pamätať.

Ubezpečujem vás, pán admirál, že na vás stále myslíme,
oceňujeme vašu službu a váš význam pre štát;
srdce vám bude prekypovať od dojatia, keď sa napokon vrátite.

Váš atď.

Absinthe Punch in Bratislava
Simon Barraclough

I have a bagful of words but they don't fit together,
like the guns and silencers in Goodfellas.
There are awkward silences.

Antigone is in town.
She's busy burying her brother in the Christmas market,
hiding his stench with pine branches.

Those are absinthe pearls that were his eyes,
rolling at the bottom of the sea-green cup.
I'm looking for trinkets for my sister.

Stone turtles reel around the fountain outside
the Slovenské národné divadlo.
I read that as diavolo. It's a devil, this lingo
and my head's still in Italy.
Snap out of it, snapping turtle.

I share an Airbnb with Ismene
and she doesn't think they're turtles at all.
What are those things Australians love to eat?
—Crayfish?
No. Bigger. Like the face-hugger in Alien.
—Oh, erm – Moreton Bay bugs?
No. They're half woman, half shellfish
and they're Cuban – Clobsters!
—Ah. I accept this as true. Why not clobsters?

On stage, a blind folk singer sings a cappella.
Between songs, his blind wife delivers lectures.
This one is on revolutionary velvet
or the legal innovations of Hungarian kings.
I can't know. The line of Hungarian kings confuses me.
Ismene read the panels in the Old Town Hall
but my eyes, in stop-motion, crawled down my cheeks into my cup.

There's a stall nearby that's a diorama of Mars.
Red earth made from red cabbage.
Red earth studded with duck legs.
A meteor shower of duck legs has hit the red planet.
There's no atmosphere, so the duck legs get through.
They call it the Great Duck-Leg Extinction.
Ismene says the air is so clean here
that mistletoe grows, naturally, everywhere.
Look!

From our room we hear the blue church levitate.
It looks like a decorated sugar cake but it moves like a Roomba
through quiet streets at night, drawn to blue souls,
sucking up doubt and crumbs from overbaked dreams.
The window frame trembles, the doorkeys twitch,
the fridge door flies open, the showerhead sings.
I pull the blanket to my nose and watch the violet light
seep across the floor to the foot of the bed.

Absintový punč v Bratislave
Simon Barraclough

Mám kopu slov, ale nepasujú k sebe,
ako zbrane a tlmiče v Mafiánoch.
Sú trápne tichá.

Antigona je v meste.
Má plné ruky práce s pohrebom brata na vianočných trhoch,
zakrýva jeho zápach borovicovými vetvičkami.

Toto sú absintové perly, ktoré boli jeho očami,
kotúľajúcimi sa na dne šálky zelenej ako more.
Hľadám dáke čačky pre sestru.

Kamenné korytnačky lemujú fontánu pred
Slovenským národným divadlom.
Čítam to ako diavolo. Je diabolská táto hatlanina
a ja som mysľou stále v Taliansku.
Hlavu hore, kajmanka dravá.

Zdieľam ich cez Airbnb s Isemene,
no tá si myslí, že to vôbec nie sú korytnačky.
Čo to tak radi jedia Austrálčania?
– Langusty?
Nie. Väčšie. Niečo ako tá príšera vo Votrelcovi.
– Ach, hmm, homáre?
Nie. Sú to napol ženy, napol mäkkýše
a sú z Kuby ¬– ryboraky!
Á, beriem to. Prečo nie ryboraky?

Na javisku spieva slepý spevák a capella.
Medzi piesňami má jeho slepá manželka prednášky.

Táto je o revolučnom zamate
či právnych inováciách uhorských kráľov.
To nemôžem poznať. Z línie uhorských kráľov mám zmätok.
Isemene prečítala tabule v Starom meste,
ale moje zastavené oči mi po lícach zliezli do šálky.

Neďaleko je stánok, dioráma Marsu.
Červenozem z červenej kapusty.
Červenozem pokrytá kačacími stehnami.
Meteorová spŕška kačacích stehien zasiahla červenú planétu.
Nie je tam atmosféra, takže kačacie stehná preletia.
Nazvú to Veľkým vymieraním kačacích stehien.
Vzduch, vraví Isemene, je tam taký čistý,
že imelo tam prirodzene rastie všade.
Pozri!

Z našej izby vidíme levitovať modrý kostolík.
Vyzerá ako zdobená torta, ale pohybuje sa ako robotický vysávač
nocou v tichu ulíc, ťahaný k smutným dušiam, vysávajúci
pochybnosti a omrvinky z prepečených snov.
Rám okna sa zatrasie, kľúčom vo dverách šklbne,
dvere chladničky sa rozletia, hlavica sprchy zaspieva.
Pritiahnem si deku k nosu a hľadím, ako fialové svetlo
presakuje cez dlážku k nohám postele.

Below the Tatra Mountains
Tera Vale Ragan

Before the August sun
and white hay are rolled
along the flats of green wilder,
the thorn grass is still high
enough for me to get down
deep into it.

I would want to be a locust,
to taste the green wings
of the daffodils, soft as the wool
on herds that feed along the brook,
its blue running through the blades
I lie on.

I would want to brush my legs
against their stems to hear
what melody the green can play
for the bronzed wheat and sun
flowers boughing up their necks
to the threshed sky.

And when the clouds collide,
romancing each other until the rain
bathes the mountains, I would raise
my wings to smell the pine green
of the forest where the doe
hides among the aspen.

And if I could climb
to the crest of a corn stalk,
I would want to see the change of hues on the patched earth,
a world in its wealth
of green.

Pod Tatrami
Tera Vale Ragan

Kým sa augustové slnko
a biele seno gúľajú
po plochách divej zelene,
bodliaky sú stále pre mňa
dosť vysoké na to, aby som sa do nich
vnorila.

Chcela by som byť kobylkou,
chutnať zelené krídla
narcisov, jemných ako vlna
čried, čo sa pasú pri potoku,
jej modrý beh cez steblá,
na ktorých ležím.

Chcela by som si obtierať nohy
o ich stonky, počuť,
akú melódiu vie zeleň zahrať
bronzovej pšenici a slnku
kvetom dvíhajúcim krky
k vymlátenej oblohe.

A keď sa zrazia mraky,
laškujú spolu, až kým dážď
neokúpe hory, dvihla by som
krídla a ovoňala borovicovú zeleň
lesa, kde srna
sa skrýva v osičine.

A keby som mohla vyliezť
na chochol kukuričného stebla,

chcela by som vidieť, ako sa menia farby na zaplátanej zemi,
svet vo svojom bohatstve
zelenej.

Short biographies of contributors Marián Andričík is engaged in literary studies and as translator. In 1988 - 1990 he worked as an editor of Dotyky magazine. From 1996 he taught at the University of Prešov. In 2003 he finished his PhD thesis Generic problems of translation. He is a translator of poetry, prose, plays, ra-dio plays, essays, literature. In 1993 he was awarded by Slovak Literary Fund for selecting translation of John Keats, 1996 the anthology of Beat Generation poetry, in 1997 for the translation of creation stories by Ted Hughes, in 2005 for the selection of the poetry of William Blake, in 2006 for English-Slovak and Slovak-English dictionary. Currently he is a vice-dean for research and doctoral study at the Faculty of Arts, Pavol Jozef Šafárik University in Košice. He lives with his wife and two children in Košice.

Elaine Baker is a poet, teacher and mentor. She has a passion for inspiring the next generation and works with young writers in secondary schools. Her pamphlet 'Winter with Eva' was published by V Press and her website is: www.elaine-baker.com

Matt Barnard is a writer and poet whose first full collection, Anatomy of a Whale, was published by the Onslaught Press. He has won and been placed in competitions including The Poetry Society's Hamish Canham Prize, the Bridport Prize, the Ink Tears short story competition, the Mo-maya short story competition and the Bristol Short Story prize. His work has appeared in a range of anthologies and magazines and he also edited the anthology Poems for the NHS (Onslaught Press). Matt was born in 1972 in London, where he still lives with his wife and their two sons and two dogs.

Simon Barraclough is a London-based poet and writer. His books are Los Alamos Mon Amour (2008), Bonjour Tetris (2010), Neptune Blue **(2011),** and Sunspots (2015). He is currently finalising a new collection.

Eleni Cay is a Slovakian-born poet living in the UK and Norway. Her most recent poems appeared in Acumen, Atticus Review, The Cardiff Review and Poetry Ireland Review. Eleni is known for her filmpoems, dancepoems and multimedia poetry, which have been screened at international festivals and featured on Button Poetry. Her first collection was published by Parthian Books and her second collection 'Love Algorithm' is forthcoming by Black Spring Press.

Mark Chamberlain's poetry has appeared in titles including Magma, The Hudson Review, Finished Creatures, The Financial Times, and FAKE by Corrupted Poetry. His poetry criticism has been published in The Times Literary Supplement. He has read his poetry widely, at venues and events including the Poetry Café in London, the Bowery Poetry Club in New York City, and the Artă La Uzină festival in Suceava, Romania. In 2019, he was poet-in-residence at the Inside Zone Writers' and Artists' Residency in Borsec, Romania.

Cahal Dallat, poet, musician, critic (b. Ballycastle, Co. Antrim), BBC Radio 4 Saturday Review contributor; winner of the 2017 Keats-Shelley Prize; founder/organiser of WB Yeats Bedford Park Artwork Project; 2019 joint Writer-in-Residence (with Anne-Marie Fyfe), Lenoir-Rhyne University, Hickory NC; 2018 Harry Ransom Center Research Fellow, University of Texas, Austin TX; 2017 Charles Causley Centenary Writer-in-Residence, Launceston, Cornwall. Latest poetry collection, The Year of Not Dancing (Blackstaff Press, Belfast); forthcoming Beautiful Lofty Things (Salmon Poetry, 2022). www.wbyeatsbedfordpark.com, www.cahaldallat.com

Catherine Temma Davidson grew up in Los Angeles but lives in London as a dual citizen. Author of New York Times notable novel, The Priest Faint-ed and most recently, The Orchard, she has won awards for her poetry on both sides of the Atlantic. Her two pamphlets are Inheriting the Ocean and Behind the Lines. She teaches creative writing at Regent's University and is on the board of Exiled Writers Ink, a platform for supporting refugee and immigrant writers.

SJ Fowler is a writer, poet and artist who lives in London. His work has become known internationally for exploring the potentials of innovative poetry, as well as performance, collaboration and neuropoetics. http://www.stevenjfowler.com

Anne-Marie Fyfe has published five books of poetry & a literary/travel/personal memoir, No Far Shore, Charting Unknown Waters (Seren Books, 2019). Born in Cushendall, County Antrim, she lives in London where she has run Coffee-House Poetry's readings & classes at London's Troubadour, since 1997, organises the annual Troubadour International Poetry Prize, is a Poetry Co-ordinator for the annual John Hewitt International Summer School in Armagh, is former Chair of the Poetry Society, and was 2019 Writer-in-Residence at Lenoir-Rhyne University in North Carolina. www.coffeehousepoetry.org www.annemariefyfe.com

John Glenday is the author of four collections. 'Grain' (Picador 2009) was shortlisted for the Griffin International Poetry Prize and the Ted Hughes Award and 'The Golden Mean' (Picador 2015) was shortlisted for the Saltire Scottish Poetry Book of the Year and won the 2016 Roehamp-ton Poetry Prize. His most recent publications are a limited edition art-book 'mira', (Coast to Coast to Coast 2019) and a pamphlet, 'The Firth' (Mariscat Press 2020). His Selected Poems came out with Picador in 2020.

Matthew Paul was born in New Malden, Surrey, in 1966 and lives in Rotherham, South Yorkshire. His collection, The Evening Entertainment, was published by Eyewear in 2017. Matthew is also the author of two collections of haiku – The Regulars (2006) and The Lammas Lands (2015) – and co-writer/editor (with John Barlow) of Wing Beats: British Birds in Haiku (2008), all published by Snapshot Press. He co-edited Presence haiku journal, has contributed to the Guardian's 'Country Diary' col-umn, regularly reviews poetry books and pamphlets, and blogs about poetry and other matters. @MatthewPaulPoet.

Miranda Peake is a poet and visual artist based in London. Her poems have been published in magazines including, Ambit, Bare Fiction, Oxford Poetry, Magma, The Moth and The Rialto. In 2014 she won the Mslexia Poetry Competition and in 2018 she was placed second in the Poetry and Psychoanalysis Competition. Her first pamphlet was published in Novem-ber 2019 with Live Canon. She holds an MA in Creative Writing from Royal Holloway and is part of the Hornet Press. She is also the owner of inde-pendent bookshop, Chener Books in South East London.

Robert Peake is an American-born poet living in the UK. He created the Transatlantic Poetry series, bringing poets together for live online readings and conversations. His film-poems collabora-tions have been widely screened in the US and Europe. His collec-tions are The Knowledge and Cyclone, both from Nine Arches Press.

James Ragan has authored 10 books (Grove/Atlantic, Henry Holt, Ireland's Salmon Publishing) with poems in Poetry, The Nation, NAR, Epoch, Bomb, World Lit Today, Los Angeles Times, Svetovej Literatury and 30 anthologies. Honors include 2 Honorary Ph.D's, 3 Fulbright Professorships, the Emerson Poetry Prize, 9 Pushcart nominations, a Poetry Society of America Citation, NEA Fellow-ship, London's Troubadour Poetry Prize fi-nalist, the Swan Founda-tion Humanitarian Award. His plays Commedia and Saints have been staged in the U.S, Moscow, Beijing, Athens. He's the subject of the documentary,"Flowers and Roots" (Arinafilms), awarded recognitions at 14 Film Festivals, including the Platinum Prize at the 49th Houston Film Festival.

Tera Vale Ragan is an American poet and author of Reading the Ground, winner of the Hilary Tham award, which uncovers her family's Slovakian roots. Passionate about story telling, Tera has produced documentary films, Flowers and Roots and Eworth, and the play, As Above in Los Angeles. Currently associate producer on Netflix's fantasy series, The Witcher, her previous television work includes TNT's The Last Ship, ABC's Revenge, and CBS's Code Black. Tera holds a BA in Creative Writing from USC and an MFA in Creative Writing from San Francisco State University. She lives be-tween Los Angeles, Prague and the UK.

Penny Sharman is a published poet, photographer, artist and therapist. She is inspired by wild natural landscapes and the relationships between the seen and the unseen. Penny has an MA in Creative Writing from Edge Hill University. She has had over 100 poems published in magazines such as The Interpreter's House, Strix, The North, Obsessed with Pipework, Finished Creatures, Orbis and Ink Sweat &Tears. Her pamphlet Fair Ground 2019 (Yaffle Press), first collection Swim With Me In Deep Water 2019 (Cerasus Poetry) and Penny's second collection The Day before Joy 2021from Knives Forks & Spoons Press are available to buy from her
web: www.pennysharman.co.uk

Theresa Sowerby's poetry has been published in magazines and anthologies and placed in competitions and recently won the Cannon Poets' Son-net or Not competition. She has had plays and monologues performed, including her 2020 Soundwork winner, Nora's Flood. Host of Wednesday Writers' Open Mic events, Theresa also lectures on and reviews poetry.

Ivana Štigová is a landscape architect, and freelance photographer and graphic designer. As a mother to three, she divides her time between designing new city parks and running a family farm in the beautiful northern Slovakia.

Christina Thatcher is a Creative Writing Lecturer at Cardiff Metropolitan University. She keeps busy off campus as Poetry Editor for The Cardiff Review, a tutor for The Poetry School, a member of the Literature Wales Management Board and as a freelance workshop facilitator across the UK. Her poetry and short stories have featured in over 50 publications including The London Magazine, Magma, North American Review, Planet Magazine, The Interpreter's House and more. She has published two poetry collections with Parthian Books: More than you were (2017) and How to Carry Fire (2020). To learn more about Christina's work please visit her website: christinathatcher.com or follow her on Twitter @writetoempower

Mark Niel is a performance poet, actor, playwright and singer/guitarist with Folk Trio 'Noah's Cape'. Mark's background is in community theatre where he started writing sketches and plays. Discovering performance poetry allowed him to combine his performance and writing skills. This led to him winning many poetry slams and performances at mainstage festivals. Mark has been the official Poet Laureate of his home town Mil-ton Keynes since 2011.

Global Slovakia is an NGO and a publishing house. It strives to raise aware-ness of Slovakia on the global stage through exceptional publications and education campaigns. The young but ambitious organization was estab-lished in 2017 and has already published 4 unique bilingual books. While their focus remains on the original production of educational literature, authored by the NGO's founders, Global Slovakia is also keen to promote the work of Slovak authors to an international audience.

At the same time, the organization is equally engaged in initiatives that help Slovakia build bridges with its vast diaspora across the world - contributing to a cultural revival that gives a new and fresh meaning to what it means to be Slovak. Global Slovakia's domestic focus is to help build a healthy civil society by working predominantly with Slovak youth, to stir their positive interest and pride in Slovakia.

www.ingramcontent.com/pod-product-compliance
Lightning Source LLC
Chambersburg PA
CBHW040421100526
44589CB00021B/2790